Evelyn Mendoza

Mother Nature's Kiss
Part- I

A coloring book inspired by mother nature herself.

This book is dedicated to everyone who never gave up on me.

To Sai and Liesl who inspired me to make this book happen.

To my birds Royce and Snowflake. I miss you.

To my college friends.

To Trio at Pierce College.

And you.

Love you guys.

Dear book buyer,

There is no wrong way of coloring this book. Color this book pretty. Color outside the lines. Color inside the lines. Color it blue, color it green, and color it with the colors of pride. For there are no rules.

Sincerely, Evelyn Mendoza

P.S. There will be more in the future.

About the Author

Evelyn Mendoza is currently a college student studying at Pierce College in Washington. Planning to graduate in 2019, then transferring to University of Washington Tacoma to get her Bio-med Bachelor's degree. Finally applying to Washington State University in Pullman for vet school. She can be found on Instagram @Djdurtdurdur.

EM
2018